T0419446

discover more
World Religions

What Is Buddhism?

Ernest Brazzos

IN ASSOCIATION WITH

Published in 2026 by Britannica Educational Publishing (a trademark of Encyclopædia Britannica, Inc.) in association with The Rosen Publishing Group, Inc.
2544 Clinton Street, Buffalo, NY 14224

Distributed exclusively by Rosen Publishing.
To see additional Britannica Educational Publishing titles, go to rosenpublishing.com.

Portions of this work were originally authored by Katy Brennan and published as *Buddhism*. All new material in this edition was authored by Ernest Brazzos.

Editor: Greg Roza
Book Design: Michael Flynn

Photo Credits: Cover Nikki Zalewski/Shutterstock.com; (series background) Dai Yim/Shutterstock.com; p. 4 Azay photography/Shutterstock.com; p. 5 Yingna Cai/Shutterstock.com; p. 6 9nong/Shutterstock.com; p. 7 Kach233/Shutterstock.com; p. 8 Romankonovalov/Shutterstock.com; p. 9 Aipon/Shutterstock.com; p. 10 Alexander Verevkin/Shutterstock.com; p. 11 A3pfamily/Shutterstock.com; p. 13 (top) cowardlion/Shutterstock.com; p. 13 (bottom) PICHAYANON PAIROJANA/Shutterstock.com; p. 14 rokaya.studio/Shutterstock.com; p. 15 PhotopankPL/Shutterstock.com; p. 17 (top) Nukul Chanada/Shutterstock.com; p. 17 (bottom) Akella Srinivas Ramalingaswami/Shutterstock.com; p. 18 PradeepGaurs/Shutterstock.com; p. 19 jejim/Shutterstock.com; p. 20 AnilD/Shutterstock.com; p. 21 Sumith Nunkham/Shutterstock.com; p. 23 (top) Anna Yordanova/Shutterstock.com; p. 23 (bottom) kazoka/Shutterstock.com; p. 24 CravenA/Shutterstock.com; p. 25 kan Sangtong/Shutterstock.com; p. 26 cowardlion/Shutterstock.com; p. 27 Somroek Anansitthichok/Shutterstock.com; p. 28 JHVEPhoto/Shutterstock.com; p. 29 Salvacampillo/Shutterstock.com.

Library of Congress Cataloging-in-Publication Data

Names: Brazzos, Ernest, author.
Title: What is Buddhism? / Ernest Brazzos.
Description: [Buffalo] : Britannica Educational Publishing, [2026] |
    Series: Discover more: world religions | Includes bibliographical
    references and index.
Identifiers: LCCN 2025010924 (print) | LCCN 2025010925 (ebook) | ISBN
    9781641904551 (library binding) | ISBN 9781641904544 (paperback) | ISBN
    9781641904568 (ebook)
Subjects: LCSH: Buddhism--Juvenile literature. | Buddhists--Juvenile
    literature.
Classification: LCC BQ4032 .B739 2026 (print) | LCC BQ4032 (ebook) | DDC
    294.3--dc23/eng/20250312
LC record available at https://lccn.loc.gov/2025010924
LC ebook record available at https://lccn.loc.gov/2025010925

Manufactured in the United States of America

Some of the images in this book illustrate individuals who are models. The depictions do not imply actual situations or events.

CPSIA Compliance Information: Batch #CSBRIT26. For further information contact Rosen Publishing at 1-800-237-9932.

Find us on

Contents

Seeking Enlightenment

Buddhism is the religion based on the teachings of the Buddha. The Buddha was born Siddhartha Gautama in what is now Nepal sometime in the sixth to the fourth century BCE, about 2,500 years ago. He became **enlightened** and found a way to free himself from the cycle of desire and suffering that all living beings experience. The Buddha taught his followers how to achieve this, too.

Statues of the Buddha are very popular in countries where the religion is popular. This 130-foot-high (40 m) statue is located in Buddha Park of Ravangla in South Sikkim, India.

There are about 4.2 million Buddhists in the United States. This Buddhist shrine is located in Woodstock, New York.

Buddhism began in India and spread to central and southeastern Asia, China, Korea, and Japan. Today, Buddhism is the fourth-largest religion in the world, with about 506 million followers, or Buddhists.

WORD WISE
ENLIGHTENED MEANS TO REACH A STATE OF TOTAL FREEDOM FROM SADNESS AND SUFFERING.

Four Noble Truths

All Buddhists share beliefs based on the teachings of the Buddha, although there is no sacred book of Buddhism. The Buddha's teachings are called the Four Noble Truths. The first truth is that life is made up of pain and suffering: all living things experience sickness, old age, and death. The second truth is that this suffering is caused by a person's selfish desires, or wants. The third truth is that people can be free of these desires. The fourth truth is that the way to overcome pain and suffering is through the Eightfold Path.

Buddhists believe they can overcome pain and suffering just as the Buddha was able to by following the Buddha's teachings.

This is a representation of samsara. It contains 6 sections in a circular order to depict the circular nature of life.

Buddhists believe in a concept called samsara. This includes the cycle of birth, death, and reincarnation, or rebirth.

Consider This

Have you ever got something you really wanted but then felt bad about getting it? Why do you think you felt unhappy?

The goal of life, according to Buddhism, is to escape from this cycle—to stop being born as an individual with selfish desires. Escape from the cycle of birth, death, and rebirth is called nirvana. In Buddhism, the way to achieve nirvana is by following the Eightfold Path.

The dharma wheel, shown here, is a symbol for the Eightfold Path. The eight spokes stand for eight practices to follow in life.

"I take refuge in the Buddha. I take refuge in the dharma. I take refuge in the sangha."

Buddhism has three main parts. These parts are called the Triratna, or "the three jewels." The first jewel is the Buddha, or the teacher. The second jewel is the dharma, or the teachings. The third jewel is the sangha, or the community of believers. Buddhist followers believe that the three jewels protect them in the world. This is expressed in a special Buddhist prayer recited by Buddhists.

Consider This

Buddhists use the word "jewel" to refer to their beliefs. Why do you think that is?

The Middle Way

The Eightfold Path teaches that people should not have too much luxury and pleasure in their lives, but they should also not go without all comforts. Instead, people should follow a middle, or balanced, course in their lives. For this reason, the Eightfold Path is also called the Middle Way.

The dharma wheel is a very common symbol in Buddhist culture and communities.

Being kind and respectful to others is an important concept in Buddhist teachings.

The first step in the Eightfold Path is Right Knowledge, and knowledge of the Four Noble Truths is part of this. The second step is Right **Aspiration**, a person's commitment to following the Eightfold Path. The third step is Right Speech, which involves speaking kindly and meaning what you say. The fourth step is Right Behavior. This step includes laws that forbid bad behavior such as lying, stealing, and killing.

WORD WISE
AN ASPIRATION IS A STRONG DESIRE TO ACHIEVE SOMETHING IMPORTANT OR GREAT.

The fifth step, Right Livelihood, involves choosing a job that supports life and goodness, rather than making a lot of money. Right Effort is the sixth step. It involves stopping one's selfish wants. The seventh step is Right Mindfulness, or being aware of one's thoughts. Right Concentration is the final goal of the Eightfold Path—to be in a state of nirvana. Not everyone can reach the goal of nirvana, but every practicing Buddhist is at least on the path toward enlightenment.

One of the most important Buddhist practices is meditation. The final goal of meditation is to achieve nirvana. Meditation is a way to make one's mind calm and peaceful by focusing on one's breathing and sitting quietly and still.

Many statues of the Buddha depict him deep in meditation.

compareandcontrast

Is meditation the same thing as prayer? How are the two different or the same?

When meditating, many Buddhist sit in a traditional, relaxing pose with legs folded and hands in the lap.

13

Who Was the Buddha?

There are many stories about the Buddha, but little is actually known about Siddhartha Gautama's life. He was said to have been a prince in a noble family. He grew up in a palace, away from aging, sickness, or death.

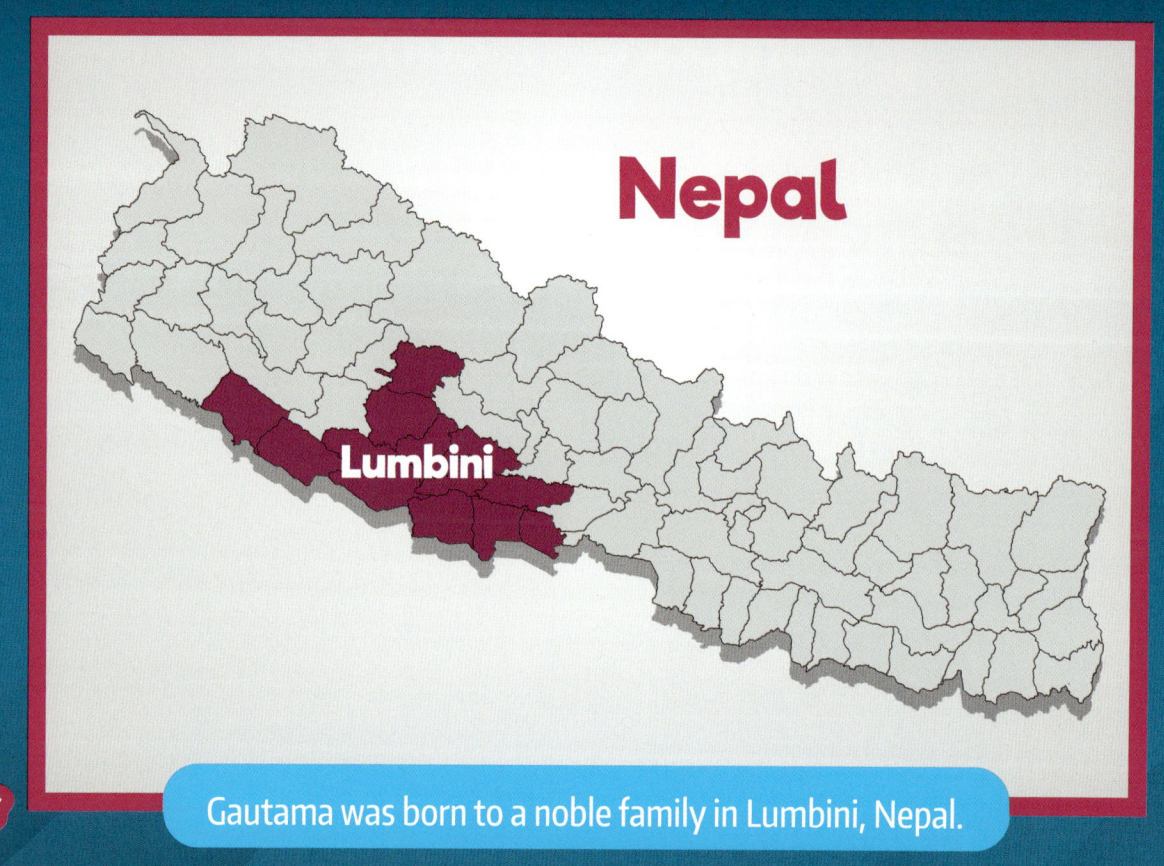

Nepal

Lumbini

Gautama was born to a noble family in Lumbini, Nepal.

Many Buddhists travel to Lumbini to visit the birthplace of the Buddha. Lumbini has many Buddhist temples and monuments.

At age twenty-nine, Gautama left the palace for the first time. Outside the palace, he saw a bent old man. This greatly troubled him. His chariot driver, Channa, explained that the man was old and that all people grow old. On another day, Gautama saw a sick man. Later he saw a dead body. Channa explained that all people experience sickness and death. Finally, Gautama saw a **monk**, who looked peaceful. He wanted to learn how the monk could be so peaceful when he was surrounded by suffering. Gautama decided to give up his wealth and become a monk.

WORD WISE

A MONK IS A MALE MEMBER OF A RELIGIOUS COMMUNITY WHOSE MEMBERS DEVOTE THEIR LIVES TO RELIGION. THEY OFTEN LIVE APART FROM SOCIETY.

One day, while Gautama was sitting and meditating under a tree, he became enlightened—free from desire and suffering. In this way, he became the Buddha, which means, "enlightened one." Soon after his enlightenment, the Buddha began sharing what he learned. He attracted followers, who became the first Buddhist order, or sangha. The Buddha sent them out into the world to spread his message. The Buddha himself set out traveling, converting many people on the way.

The Buddha did not write down his teachings. He preached in Pali, which was the language of the common people. His followers shared his teachings with other people by word of mouth. These teachings were not put in writing until many years after the Buddha's death.

This location in Bodh Gaya, India, is where Gautama meditated and found enlightenment. It is now a Buddhist temple.

compareandcontrast

The Buddha is said to have founded Buddhism. How is the Buddha similar to other religious founders, such as Jesus (Christianity) and Mohammad (Islam)? How are they different?

The Buddha lived until he was 80. Shown here is a stupa—a Buddhist monument—that was built over the place where the Buddha was cremated. It is located in Kushinagar, India.

17

Spreading Around the World

The monks in the Buddha's sangha helped spread Buddhism throughout northern India. In the 200s BCE, King Ashoka, an important ruler of an empire that covered most of South Asia, became Buddhist. He built many Buddhist monuments and **monasteries**. Because of King Ashoka, Buddhism spread throughout all of India.

This statue of King Ashoka is displayed in Shaheedi Park, an outdoor museum in Delhi, India.

Since the sixth century, Buddhism has continued to spread around the world. The City of Ten Thousand Buddhas, shown here in Talmage, California, was one of the first Buddhist temples in the United States.

Beginning in the second century CE, trade bought Indian people and ideas into China. Buddhist monks traveled with the traders and spread Buddhism to China. Buddhism became the most popular religion in China in the fourth and fifth centuries. Buddhism spread to Korea in the fourth century and to Japan in the sixth century.

WORD WISE
A MONASTERY IS A HOME FOR PEOPLE WHO HAVE TAKEN RELIGIOUS VOWS.

Breaking Down Buddhism

In time, two major groups appeared among the Buddha's followers. Today, within the two major branches of Buddhism, there are many smaller schools of Buddhism throughout Asia. These schools have different writings and languages and have grown up in different cultures.

The Pali Canon is a collection of Buddhist writings. Many years ago, the Pali Canon was printed on thin strips of wood, and not in book format.

Zen Buddhism is a division of Mahayana Buddhism. It focusing particularly on meditation.

One of the two major groups is known as Theravada, meaning "Way of the Elders." It is the older and more conservative branch of Buddhism. Many people in Sri Lanka, Myanmar, Thailand, Laos, and Cambodia belong to this group. The Theravada Buddhists concentrate on freeing themselves through improving their own lives.

The other major group is called Mahayana. Mahayana Buddhism is popular in Mongolia, China, Japan, Korea, Vietnam, and Nepal. Mahayana Buddhists believe they can achieve enlightenment through a life of good work for others. After becoming enlightened, Mahayana Buddhists help others reach enlightenment.

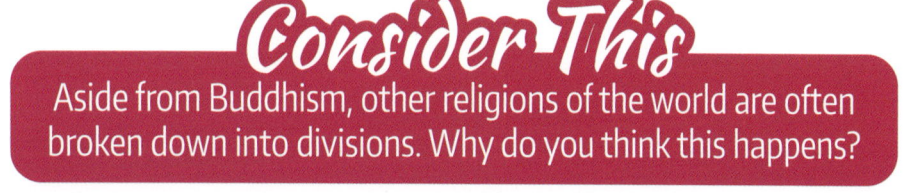

Consider This

Aside from Buddhism, other religions of the world are often broken down into divisions. Why do you think this happens?

Buddhist Temples

A Buddhist place of worship is called a temple. Buddhist temples look different depending on where they are in the world, but all Buddhist temples have an image or a statue of the Buddha. Worshippers may sit on the floor and chant prayers or listen to monks chant. At home, Buddhists worship in front of a shrine. A Buddhist shrine has a statue or picture of the Buddha. Buddhists may bring offerings of fruit or flowers and place them on the shrine. Buddhists light candles and incense while they sit quietly to worship.

Monasteries are places for monks and nuns to live, work, study, and pray. In Theravada Buddhism, monks and nuns live away from society in their monasteries. In Mahayana Buddhism, monks and nuns vow to help the larger community to which they belong. Buddhist monks and nuns use prayer, meditation, and other rituals to stay on the Eightfold Path.

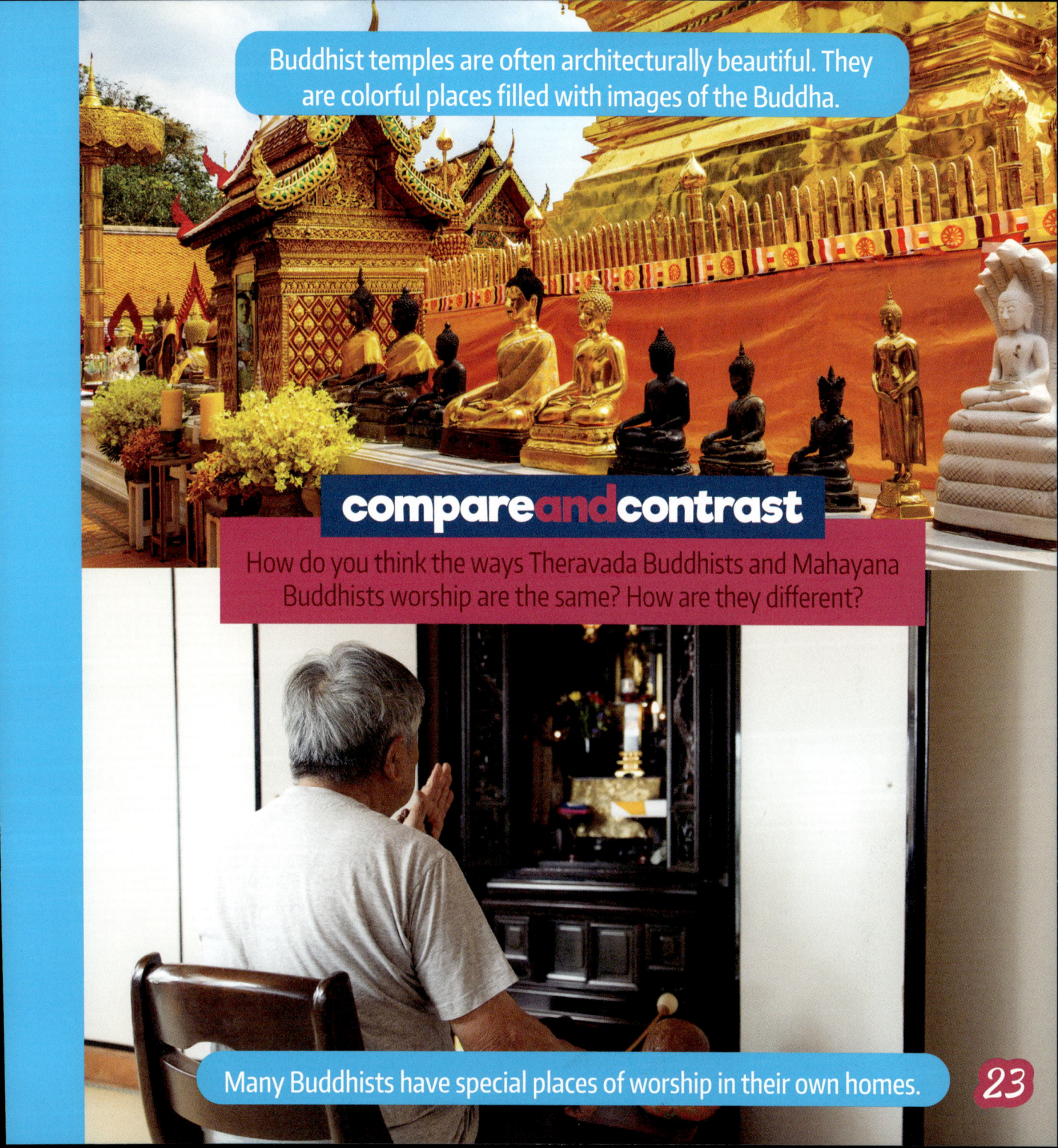

Buddhist temples are often architecturally beautiful. They are colorful places filled with images of the Buddha.

compare and contrast

How do you think the ways Theravada Buddhists and Mahayana Buddhists worship are the same? How are they different?

Many Buddhists have special places of worship in their own homes.

Let's Celebrate!

Buddhists have many yearly celebrations. The three major events of the Buddha's life—his birth, enlightenment, and death—are commemorated by every Buddhist, but not always on the same day.

Buddhist festivals are often celebrated differently by Theravada and Mahayana Buddhists. Theravada Buddhists celebrate the Buddha's life events together on Vesak, which is also called Wesak, Buddha Purnima, Buddha Jayanti, or Vaishaka Purnima. Vesak occurs on a full moon, usually in April.

Vietnamese Buddhists celebrate Tet, or Lunar New Year, in January or February each year. Many people in Vietnam also celebrate this holiday even though they aren't Buddhist. Tet celebrations often include fireworks.

Buddhists in East Asia celebrate the Buddha's birthday on the first full moon of Vesak.

Theravada Buddhists also celebrate four days every month as uposatha days. These special days are the new moon (when the moon is dark in the night sky), the full moon, and the eighth day after each new and full moon. On uposatha days, Theravada Buddhists gather to meditate, hear sermons, recite **sutras**, and make offerings.

WORD WISE
SUTRAS ARE THE TEACHINGS OF THE BUDDHA.

Theravada Buddhists also practice vassa, a three month retreat during the rainy season, from July to October. During vassa, a person lives like a monk for a short time. A big celebration takes place at the end of vassa.

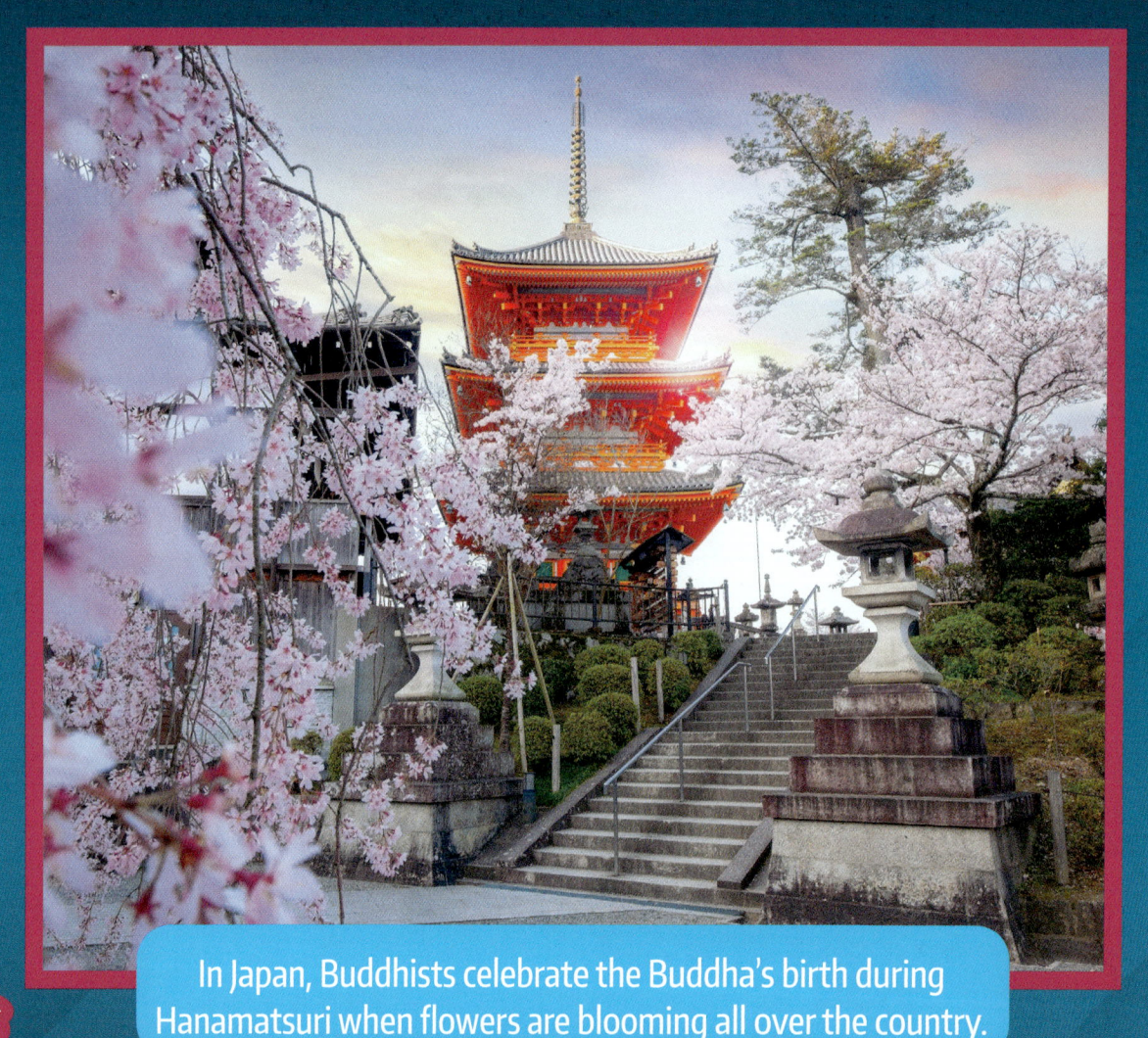

In Japan, Buddhists celebrate the Buddha's birth during Hanamatsuri when flowers are blooming all over the country.

People put out bowls of fruit and flowers during All Souls Festival as an offering to the Buddha.

Mahayana Buddhists celebrate the life events of the Buddha on three separate days. They remember the Buddha's birth on April 8. In Japan, the celebration of the Buddha's birth is part of a flower festival known as Hanamatsuri. Mahayana Buddhists remember the Buddha's enlightenment on December 8 and his death on February 15.

Buddhists also celebrate New Year's and harvest festivals according to local customs and traditions. In China and Japan, Buddhists have a holiday when people remember the dead and pray to bring them peace. This is called All Souls Festival.

Consider This

Why do you think so many cultures have festivals to celebrate the New Year?

Modern Buddhism

Western thinkers began to embrace Buddhism in the nineteenth century. Buddhist principles of generosity, kindness, and wisdom appeal to many Westerners who adopted the religion. Also in the nineteenth century, Asian immigrants brought Buddhism to the United States. Today, many Buddhist communities exist throughout the United States. As much as it changed to fit new cultures in the past, Buddhism adapts to fit American culture. There are more than three million Buddhists in North America today.

This statue of the Buddha can be found at the Buddhist Place in Peterborough, Ontario, where members of the community can learn about Buddhism.

Tenzin Gyatso is the fourteenth Dalai Lama of Tibetan Buddhism.

Buddhism is a thriving religion, with its center in Asia. Perhaps the most famous Buddhist in the world is the Dalai Lama, a Tibetan Buddhist leader. The Dalai Lama travels the world and shares the Buddha's message of peace with everyone he meets.

Consider This

Why do you think Buddhism has become popular throughout the world in the past 100 years? Why wasn't it more popular in the West years ago?

Glossary

chariot A wheeled vehicle for passengers that is pulled by horses.

commemorate To mark by a ceremony.

conservative Holding on to older, more traditional ideas.

convert To cause someone to adopt a new religion.

cycle Something that repeats.

desire A strong wish.

empire A major political power with control over a large area.

generosity The quality of giving unselfishly.

incense Something that is burnt to make a pleasant smell in the air.

luxury Great ease or comfort; rich surroundings.

monument An important structure that is built as a memorial.

noble Having a high rank in society or having qualities of a high moral character.

order A group of people who share religious beliefs.

preach To speak about religious ideas to a group of people.

refuge Shelter or protection from harm.

sacred Holy; something important to a particular religion.

suffering The feeling of pain.

wisdom Knowledge.

For More Information

Books

Robeson, Teresa. *Who Is Tibet's Exiled Leader? The 14th Dalai Lama.* London, UK: Penguin Workshop, 2023.

Shey, Sarah. *Buddhist Festivals and Traditions.* Mankato, MN: Capstone, 2025.

Websites

Buddha Quotes

wisdomquotes.com/buddha-quotes
Read a collection of simple yet thought-provoking quotes that are attributed to the Buddha.

Buddhism and the Buddha for Kids

ancienthistory.mrdonn.org/Buddhism.html
Read more about Buddhism and the Buddha. Includes links to more resources.

Index